Like All But Me

Für Luca, Moritz und Charlotte

Like all but me
—Ich bin wie alle und doch besonders

Fotografien von Carolin Schüten. Mit einem Text von Vera King

Max, 12 USA

Blanca, 12 Spain

Ariel, 10 Israel

Asram, 12 Sudan

Carlos, 13 Spain

Romy, 12 USA

Michael, 11 Israel

Johan, 12 Spain

Paul, 11 Germany

Jona, 12 Germany

Hedda, 13 Germany

Lira, 10 Brazil

Salim, 11 Germany

Charlotte, 10 Germany

Ludwig, 11 Germany

Jina-Yi, 11 USA

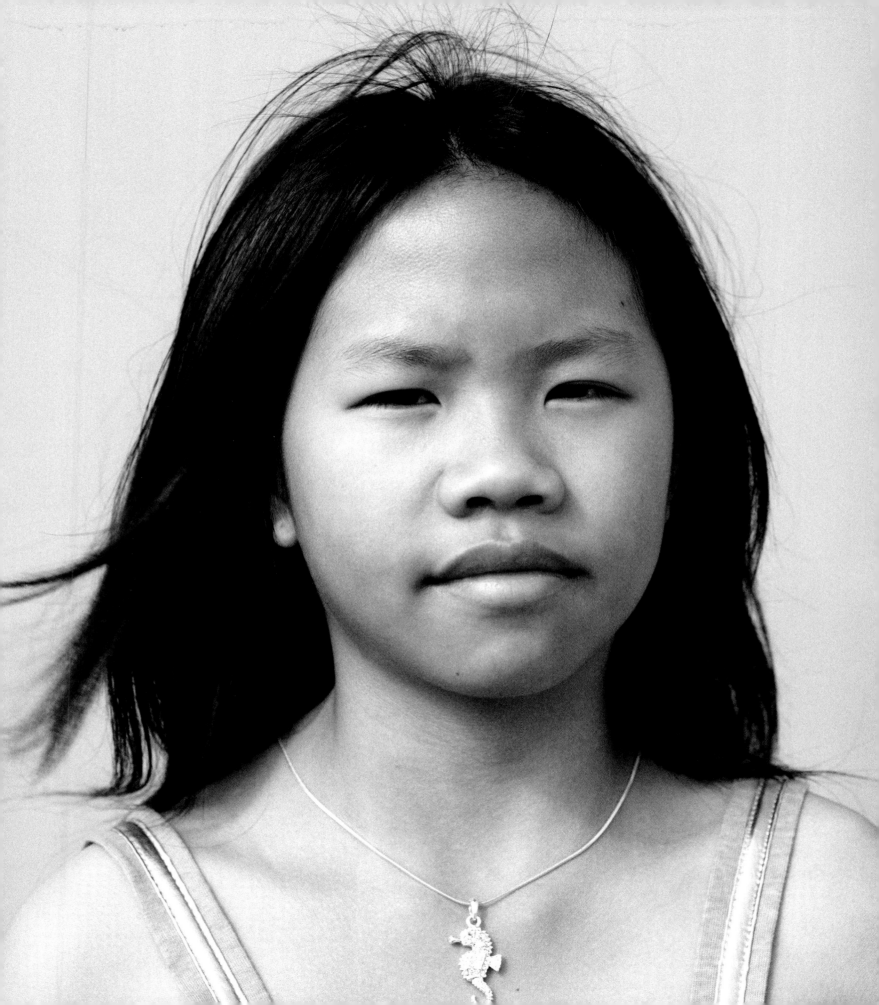

Philippa, 11 Germany

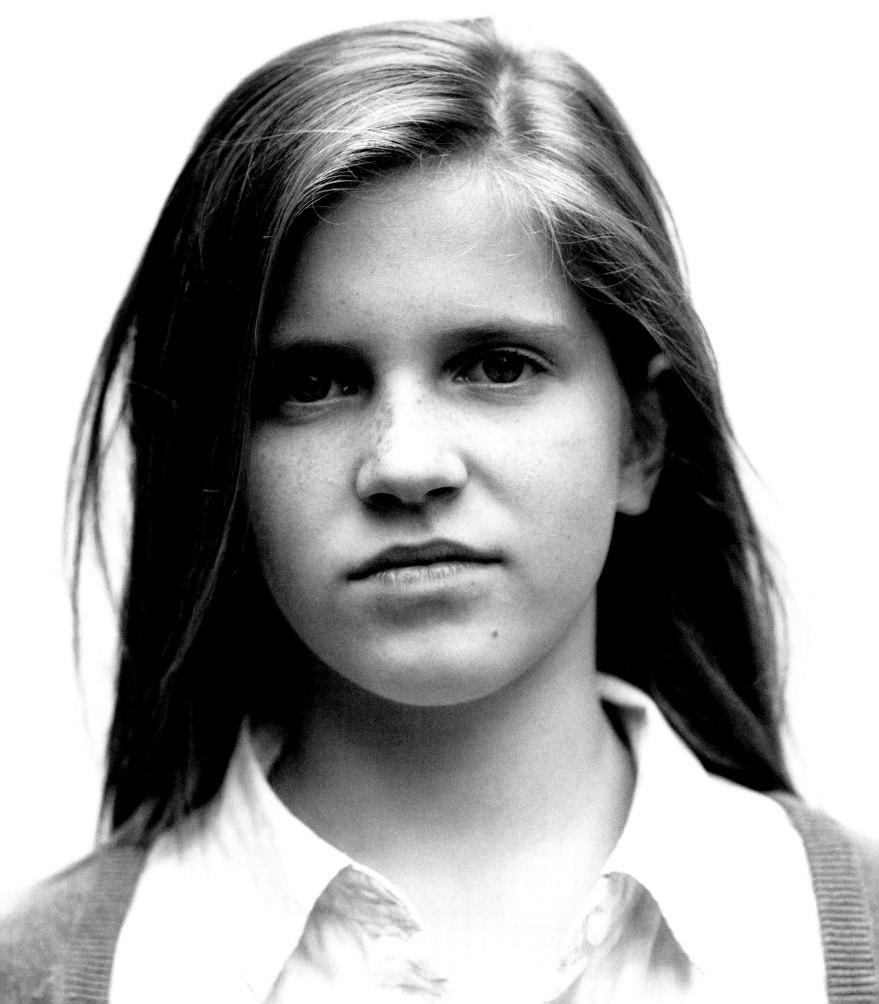

Achmed, 12 Sudan

Jordi, 11 Spain

Yossef, 11 Israel

Cody, 12 USA / **Luca, 11** Germany

Vera King
—Erwachen des Selbst

*Bilder eines besonderen Moments
am Ende der Kindheit*

Die Photographien dieses Bandes von Carolin Schüten zeigen Portraits von Heranwachsenden zwischen 10 und 14 Jahren, die beim Betrachten unmittelbar berühren durch ihre ungewöhnliche Ernsthaftigkeit und eigensinnige Kraft. Dabei wirft jedes Bild ein besonderes Licht auf den Übergang von der Kindheit zur Jugend. So erscheinen die Photographien als Ausdrucksformen eines spezifischen, geradezu einmaligen lebensgeschichtlichen Moments: Die Naivität der Kindheit ist bereits abgestreift und ein neues Bewusstsein seiner selbst und der Welt erlangt. Zugleich ist in ihnen noch eine Unverstelltheit erhalten, die bald darauf für einige Zeit vom jugendlichen Sich-in-Szene-setzen und Gefallenwollen verdeckt sein wird – und doch auch subtil weiterwirken kann.

‚Seelenbilder' – ohne Pose

Man könnte sagen, die Bilder halten in erstaunlicher Prägnanz etwas fest, das im günstigen Fall im Entwicklungsprozess der Adoleszenz, der Lebensphase zwischen Kindheit und Erwachsenheit, als ein kostbarer innerer Schatz bewahrt wird. Sie fokussieren auf überraschende Weise etwas in diesem Moment deutlich Präsentes, im Ansatz schon Flüchtiges. Etwas, das später in die erwachsene Identität als ein Kern der Wahrhaftigkeit auf neue Weise integriert werden kann. Oder aber es geht verloren und bleibt dann verhüllt von den vielfältigen Bemühungen im Erwachsenenleben, sich selbst ins rechte Licht zu rücken, Eindruck zu machen. In der Mimik dieser groß gewordenen Kinder verdichtet sich hingegen ein ernsthaftes, weitgehend noch unverstelltes Bei-sich-sein auf je unterschiedliche Weise. Ich kann mich nicht erinnern, eine vergleichbare Arbeit, eine solche Bebilderung dieses ‚Umschlagsmoments' je gesehen zu haben. Die Photographien berühren wie ‚Seelenbilder', in denen die Mädchen und Jungen sich zeigen, ohne zu posieren.

Verletzlichkeit und Vertrauen in die Zukunft – die Welt als Hülle

Besonders eindrücklich ist dabei, dass sich diese humane Kostbarkeit offenkundig in so vielen verschiedenen Kontexten, Ländern und Regionen festhalten ließ. So wird unmittelbar

Awakening the Self—Images of a Singular Moment at the End of Childhood

The subjects of Carolin Schüten's photographic portraits collected in this volume are all adolescents between the ages of 10 and 14. The uncommon intensity and self-contained strength of these images, each casting a unique light on the moment of transition from childhood to early adulthood, strikes the viewer immediately. We become witnesses to a singular moment of biographical transition, when the naiveté of childhood has been stripped away and a new awareness of the self and of the outside world has taken its place. Yet these faces retain an authenticity unique to childhood, one that continues to subtly affect self-understanding though it may be obscured, at least for a time, by a variety of postures taken up out of the desire for acceptance.

Pictures of the Soul

With remarkable concision, these images capture something that, in the best case, will be preserved as a precious inner treasure throughout the process of becoming adult. They bring to focus in unexpected ways something in this transitional moment that is distinctly present, yet essentially fleeting— a core of truthfulness that may become part of adult identity, or that is lost in adult life, veiled by the array of efforts to show oneself in the best light, to make an impression. Concentrated in the faces of each of these grown-up children we sense a serious, principally unpretentious self-possession. These portraits are like none I have seen before. They are "pictures of the soul," in which these young girls and boys reveal themselves before the camera without affectation.

Vulnerability and Faith in the Future—The World as Chrysalis

This series of portraits is remarkable not only for the candor of its subjects but, in particular, for having captured this unique transitional moment in so many different contexts, countries and regions of the world. These photographs thus bear witness, on the one hand, to the universality of this moment at the same time they document its uniqueness for each of these subjects. The images make it apparent that different social, physical and economic environments—and

deutlich, dass unterschiedliche Umgebungsbedingungen auf die Jugendlichen in ihrem Prozess des Großwerdens eingewirkt haben. Dass sie die damit verbundenen Chancen und Bürden auf ihrer eigenen Reise ins Erwachsenwerden mitnehmen. In ihren Blicken vermitteln sie etwas von ihrer Geschichte und der sie umgebenden Welt. Die Jugendlichen sind im Aufbruch, halten noch einen Moment inne und der Betrachter ist aufgefordert, sich hineinzuversetzen und innerlich mitzugehen. So wirken die Bilder auch wie eine Verheißung, die Einfühlung, Spannung und Neugierde erzeugt. Beim Betrachten ergibt sich ein facettenreiches Panorama von lebensgeschichtlich bedeutsamen Themen des Heranwachsens, die hier nur angedeutet werden können.

Wer ich bin oder sein könnte …

Die in Teilen bereits gebahnte, teils noch offene Zukunft des eigenen Werdens spiegelt sich in Ausdruck und Mimik der Portraitierten. Einschneidende Veränderungen dieser Zeit spiegeln sich im Blick der Heranwachsenden. Denn am Ende der Kindheit verändert sich die Wahrnehmung der eigenen Person und der Anderen. Jugendliche entwickeln im Zuge dessen auch ein verändertes Gespür für Grenzen. Sie sind sensibilisiert auch für eine Begrenztheit, die als Herausforderung erlebt und zu überwinden versucht werden kann. Es entstehen neue Formen der Selbstbetrachtung und der Beschäftigung mit der eigenen Identität. Die Fragen Wer bin ich? Woher komme ich? Wohin gehe ich? erlangen eine herausragende Bedeutung. Das lang Bekannte, elterliche Erwartungen oder bisher gültige Regeln verlieren ihre Selbstverständlichkeit. Zugleich können sich Anpassung und Rebellion, Niedergeschlagenheit und Triumph rasch abwechseln. Wechselnde Pfade werden eingeschlagen und wieder verlassen. Zeitweilige Orientierungsverluste können verstärkt werden durch gesellschaftlichen Wandel, wenn ehemals unverbrüchliche Lebenszusammenhänge oder auch Familienbindungen ihre Verbindlichkeit eingebüßt haben. Dabei haben Auflockerungen von Traditionen auch Wandlungen ehemals starrer Normen, etwa der Geschlechterrollen begünstigt. Heranwachsende können und müssen sich dann intensiver selbst damit auseinandersetzen, was es für sie

the opportunities and challenges arising from them—have influenced these adolescents in their developmental process, on their journey to adulthood. Their gazes convey something of their histories and backgrounds. These young people are in a process of becoming, pause for an instant before the camera, and we, as viewers of these photographic portraits, are challenged to put ourselves in their place, to walk a proverbial mile in their shoes. Like a promise, these images awaken empathy, excitement and curiosity. They encompass a spectrum of biographically significant themes related to growing up that can only be suggested here.

Who I am, or could be …

The future of their own becoming—to some extent defined, to some extent still uncertain—is reflected in the faces, expressions and gazes of the subjects. They contain the traces of intensity associated with the momentous transformations of this particular time in life, when, at the end of childhood, our perception of the self and of others changes. With new ways of seeing, adolescents develop a new sensitivity for boundaries, now perceived as challenges, as something to be overcome. Adolescents develop new ways of seeing themselves and of examining their own identities. The questions Who am I? Where do I come from? Where am I going? take on greater significance. Things long familiar, parental expectations and as-yet valid rules, all lose their a priori status. At the same time, adolescents experience conformity and rebellion, defeat and triumph in rapid alternation. They start down new paths and leave them for another. Temporary loss of orientation can be exacerbated by social transformation, when once steadfast life contexts or familial ties have lost their validity. While the less stringent hold of tradition on identity has lead to transformations in once rigid norms, such as gender roles, today's adolescents can and must struggle with this new complexity, on their own, with what it means to be a girl or a boy, to become a woman or man. Family histories, pictures of one's own origins become vital (How have I become, what am I?) when thinking of the future, as well as one's own creative potential (What will I be and bring into being?) together with the manifold hopes and

bedeutet, Mädchen oder Junge zu sein, Frau oder Mann zu werden. Familiengeschichten, Bilder über den eigenen Ursprung werden lebendig: Wie bin ich geworden, was ich bin? beim Ausmalen der Zukunft und der eigenen schöpferischen Potenz: Was werde ich selbst sein und hervorbringen? Verbunden mit vielschichtigen Hoffnungen und Lasten, die die Reise ins Ungewisse des Großwerdens prägen und einen Hintergrund der Bilder darstellen. Sie blitzen auf, in einer mitunter äußerst ausdrucksstarken Weise, in den Blicken der Portraitierten.

Riskante Aufbrüche

Denn für diese Reise der Selbstsuche gibt es gerade in modernen Gesellschaften weniger vorgezeichnete Bahnen. Übergänge in neue Lebensphasen werden dann zunehmend weniger ‚von außen', durch festgelegte Rollen oder Rituale reguliert. Sie obliegen vielmehr den Bewältigungsmöglichkeiten der Beteiligten selbst. Übergänge werden dadurch gewissermaßen ‚nach innen' verlagert, sodass individuelle Kompetenzen eine verstärkte Rolle spielen. Das Erwachsenwerden verläuft daher weder selbstverständlich, noch für alle gleich, noch konfliktlos, noch ein für alle Mal abschließbar. Im Gegenteil: Die Veränderung des Ich erzeugt phasenweise eine Art Vakuum, das jugendliches Selbständigwerden potenziell risikoreich macht. Wie groß die Entfernungen vom Vertrauten der kindlichen Welt sind, die dabei gewagt werden, hängt ebenso von dem inneren und äußeren Veränderungsdruck ab wie auch von den Ressourcen, die das Risiko erträglich machen. Das Sich-Entfernen vom sicheren Hafen ist zugleich von der Suche nach Anerkennung getrieben – aber auch vom Wunsch, sich von dieser unabhängig zu machen. Eine beunruhigende Spannung, die in den Bildern oft als vitale Kraft imponiert, mitunter auch als Ausdruck von Schmerz und bereits erfahrener Verletzung entgegentritt.

Den Kosmos der Kindheit verlassen – ungleiche Chancen

Nicht alle verfügen über die Chancen, sich zu erproben, zu experimentieren - oder haben zugleich einen einigermaßen verlässlichen Hafen. Je nach Geschlecht und Herkunft stehen beim Großwerden unterschiedliche Ressourcen und

fears that shape the journey into the unknown of becoming adult and which constitute the context of these images. They flash up, in sometimes extremely expressive ways, in the faces of these young adults.

Risky Ventures

The journey of self discovery in modern societies offers fewer and fewer worn paths. There are ever fewer predetermined roles and rituals from "outside" sources to regulate the transition to new phases of life. As such, life transitions are shifted, to a certain extent, to the "inside," so that successfully navigating them is increasingly a matter of individual competency and capacity to cope with change. The process of growing up, then, is neither a matter of course, nor is it the same for everyone; it is neither without conflict, nor is it a process that comes, finally, to an end. On the contrary, the transformation of the self creates, in phases, a kind of vacuum, making the process of adolescent independence potentially risky. Just how far adolescents dare to venture from the trusted environment of their childhood world is dependent upon both the internal and external stimulus for change, as well as the resources available to them that make the risk more bearable. Distancing oneself from safe harbors is driven, at once, by the desire for recognition, as well as by the wish to free oneself from need of this recognition—an unsettling tension visible in the images as vitality and, sometimes, as an expression of suffering and injury already experienced.

Leaving Childhood—Unequal Opportunity

Not all adolescents have the same opportunities to test and experiment—nor do they all begin from the same relatively safe harbor. Depending on their sex and origins, they have different resources and developmental space in which to unfold in the process of growing up, including detaching from parents. The psychosocial event of detachment can be understood as a three stage process involving separation, transformation, and re-creation, in which the dominant "portal figures of life," as Peter Weiss refers to the once powerful and idealized parents, are removed from their proverbial pedestals. At the same time, however, and this too makes detachment so psychically risky, the adolescents are dependent upon

Entwicklungsspielräume zur Verfügung. Dies betrifft auch das, was man Ablösung von den Eltern nennt. Das psychosoziale Geschehen der Ablösung ist verstehbar als Dreischritt von Trennung, Umgestaltung und Neuschöpfung. Dabei müssen die in der Kindheit noch dominierenden „Portalfiguren des Lebens" (Peter Weiss), die einst mächtigen und idealisierten Eltern, innerlich gleichsam von ihrem Sockel gehoben werden. Zugleich jedoch, und auch das macht Ablösung psychisch riskant, sind Heranwachsende auch im Trennungs- und Verselbständigungsprozess noch auf Erwachsene angewiesen. Obwohl sie meist anders erscheinen wollen. Großwerden ist ein störanfälliger Prozess, bei dem Adoleszente phasenweise innerlich jene attackieren müssen, auf die sie zugleich noch angewiesen sind. Eben dazu bedarf es eines Spielraums, in den die Erwachsenen nicht ihrerseits störend oder destruktiv eingreifen. Aus dieser Sicht scheinen die Gesichter der Jungen und Mädchen auch eine Anmutung an die Erwachsenen zu enthalten: Eine Aufforderung, ihnen zu vertrauen und jenen Raum zu lassen, den sie benötigen.

Augen-Blick: die Welt erkennen – Sich zeigen

So bewegen die Bilder gerade dadurch, dass die Portraitierten sich ungeschützt der Kamera preisgeben. Zugleich gibt es viele Varianten eines in sich ruhenden Stolzes, eines offenen Blicks: Den Anderen betrachten, die Welt erkennen, Sich-Zeigen sind im besten Falle eins geworden. Die Bilder halten eben diesen Augen-Blick fest. Sie fordern heraus und verführen dazu, die Vergangenheiten und Zukünfte der Heranwachsenden auszumalen. Hat doch jedes dieser großen Kinder und Jugendlichen eine ganz besondere Geschichte, in der sie Gewordene sind und geprägt von ihren Umgebungen. Die Bilder lassen Ahnungen aufblitzen, zugleich erscheinen die Mädchen und Jungen im besten Sinne singulär. In diesen Bildern stehen sie im Zentrum, sind sie zumeist dem Kosmos ihrer Kindheiten bereits Entschlüpfte. Werden sie ihr Leben eigensinnig gestalten können? Wie wird es sich in dieser Welt leben lassen, in der die älteren Generationen ihre Spuren hinterlassen haben?

these very same parents during the process of separation and self-understanding, though they often desire to appear not to be. Growing up is a process prone to disruption, in which adolescents, in phases, must inwardly attack those upon whom they are dependent. Precisely for this reason adolescents require space and time in which the parents do not interfere disruptively or destructively. Seen in this light, the faces of these boys and girls appear to contain a suggestion of adultness: An entreaty to trust them and give them the space they need.

Seeing the World—Being Seen

These images move us precisely because their subjects reveal themselves—unguarded—before the camera. Each presents a particular image of self-contained pride and openness—observing others, seeing and knowing the world, presenting oneself are all ideally united. It is this moment of seeing and being seen that these images capture. They challenge and tempt us to imagine the pasts and futures of these adolescents, each of whom has a particular history, a specific background and environment that has shaped their biographies and developmental process. The images give us flashes of insight, yet the girls and boys remain in the best sense unique. These photographs put them at the center; most of them have already left their childhoods behind. Will they be able to shape and master their lives independently? What kind of life will they be able to lead in a world bearing the traces of older generations?

Solitude and the Birth of the New—Stay Awhile

Becoming independent naturally means wrestling with imperfection, with limitations, with the painful aspects of one's own past, the peculiarities and inadequacies of parents and family, of one's origins and environment, all of which are suddenly experienced in a new light. For this reason, too, adolescence is often literally associated with the experience of loneliness and solitude. Sometimes adolescents quite concretely withdraw from their environments. Yet moments of aloneness in adolescence are important, above all, figuratively, for in essence being alone has to do with the precarious situation of transition—between no-longer-childhood and

Einsamkeit und die Entstehung des Neuen – verweile doch ….

Selbständigwerden heisst freilich immer auch Ringen mit Unvollkommenheit, mit Grenzen. Mit den schmerzlichen Seiten der eigenen Geschichte, den Besonderheiten und Unzulänglichkeiten der Eltern und Familie, der Herkunft und Umgebungen, die in verändertem Licht erfahren werden. Auch deshalb wird die Jugendphase sprichwörtlich oft mit dem Erleben von Einsamkeit verbunden. Mitunter ziehen sich Jugendliche auch ganz konkret zurück. Momente des Einsamseins sind in der Adoleszenz indes vor allem bedeutsam in einem übertragenen Sinne. Geht es doch im Kern um die prekäre Übergangssituation – zwischen dem Nicht-mehr der Kindheit und dem Noch-Nicht des Neuen. ‚Einsamkeit' resultiert demnach aus dem Verlust gewohnter Bezugspunkte. Insofern setzt Ablösung auch Ängste frei, die etwa zu rückwärtsgewandten unproduktiven Handlungen oder Haltungen verführen können. Kehrseitig ist Kreativität eben auch eine Form der Angstbewältigung, Mittel der Selbstbehauptung. Im späteren Leben der Erwachsenen kann im günstigen Fall auf diese schöpferischen Ressourcen zurückgegriffen und etwas vom ernsthaften Bei-sich-sein der Nicht-mehr-Kindheit bewahrt werden. Auch daran, nicht zuletzt, erinnern die Bilder dieses Bandes von Carolin Schüten.

the not-yet-new. 'Loneliness' derives, in this case, from the loss of familiar points of reference. Insofar, detachment produces anxiety that may lead to regressive, unproductive behaviors and attitudes. Conversely, creativity serves as a form of coping with fear, as a means of self-assertion. In later life, the adult can, ideally, take recourse to these creative resources and retain an element of childhood authenticity. It is, not least, of this that the images in Carolin Schüten's book remind us.

Stefanie, 12 Brazil

Abeer, 12 Israel

Fabio, 12 Brazil

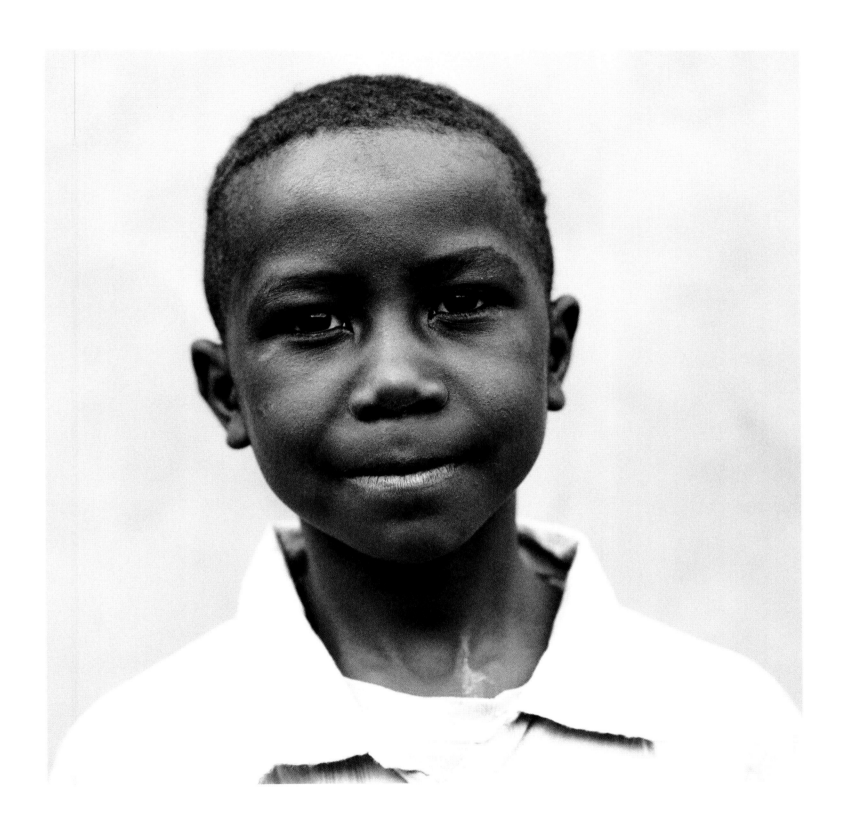

Diani, 10 Sudan

Shuk, 12 Israel

Selma, 10 Sudan

Ahed, 12 Israel

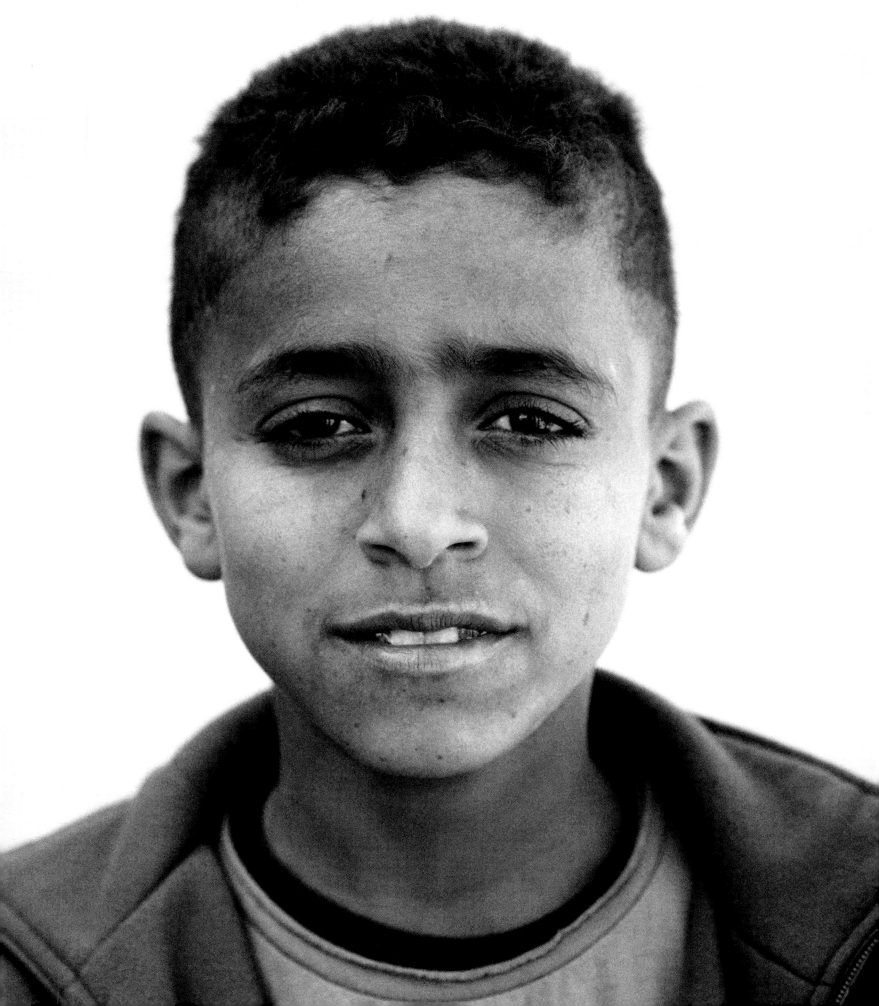

Alham, 12 Israel

Mais, 12 Israel

Mohamed, 13 Israel

Abdan, 12 Sudan

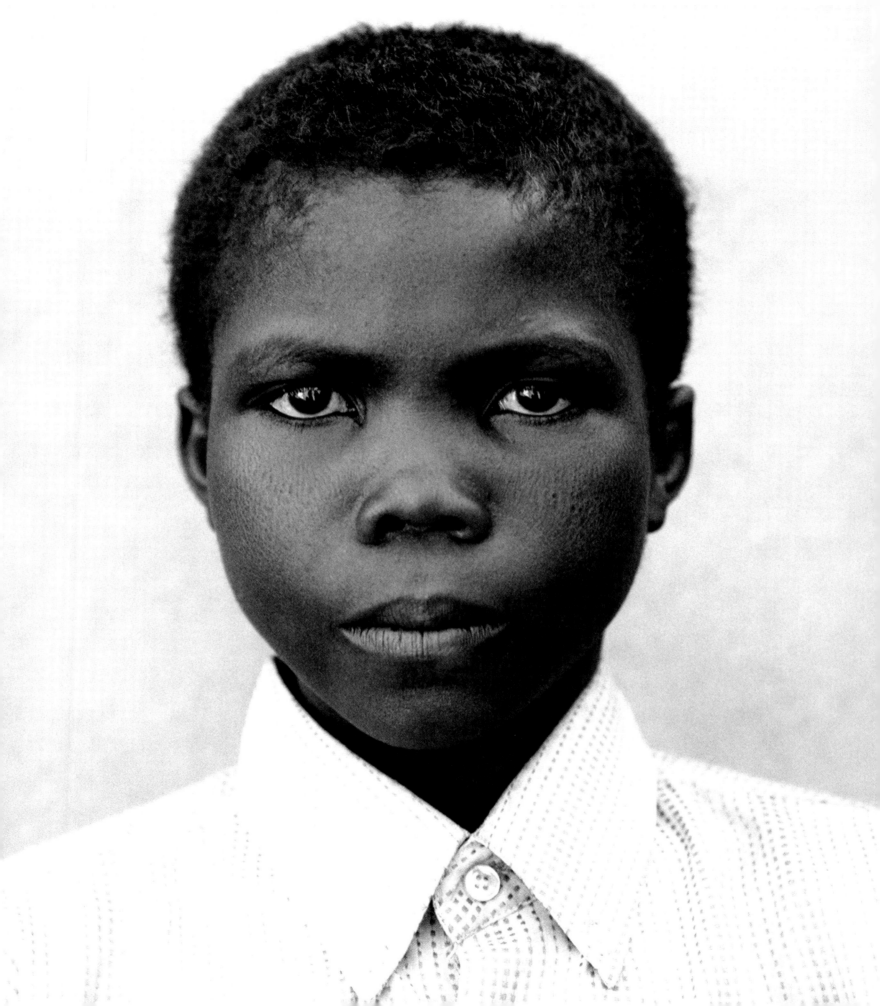

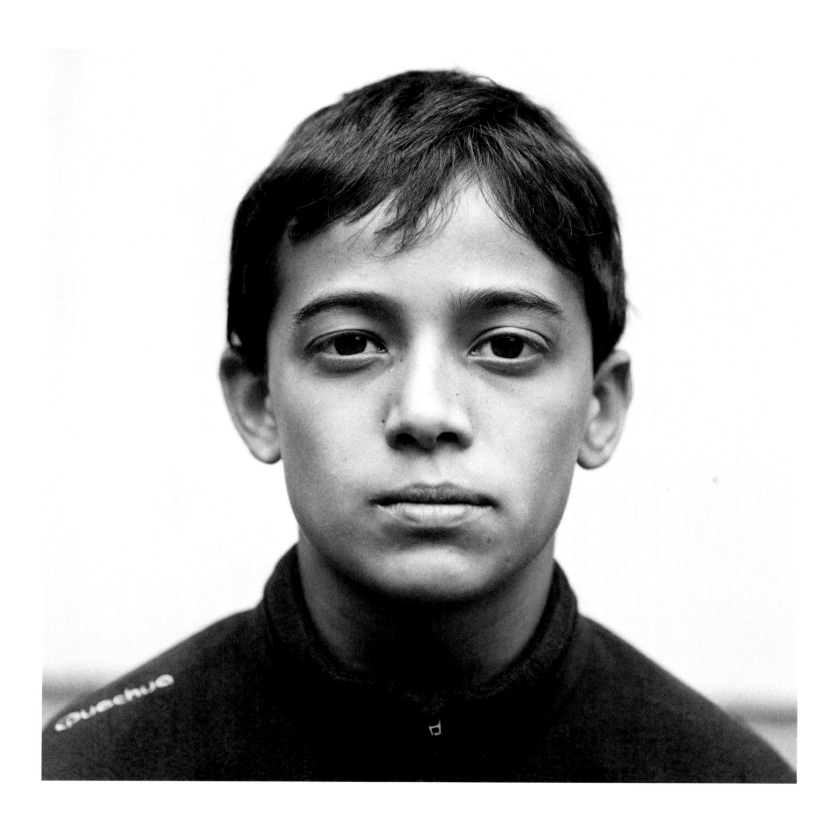

Oskar, 12 Spain

Halima, 12 Sudan

Jana, 10 Germany

Juman, 11 Israel

Alexa, 11 USA

Lara, 10 Germany

Ronnie, 12 USA

Melissah, 12 Germany

Clara, 12 Germany

I Kadek Rian, 12 Indonesia

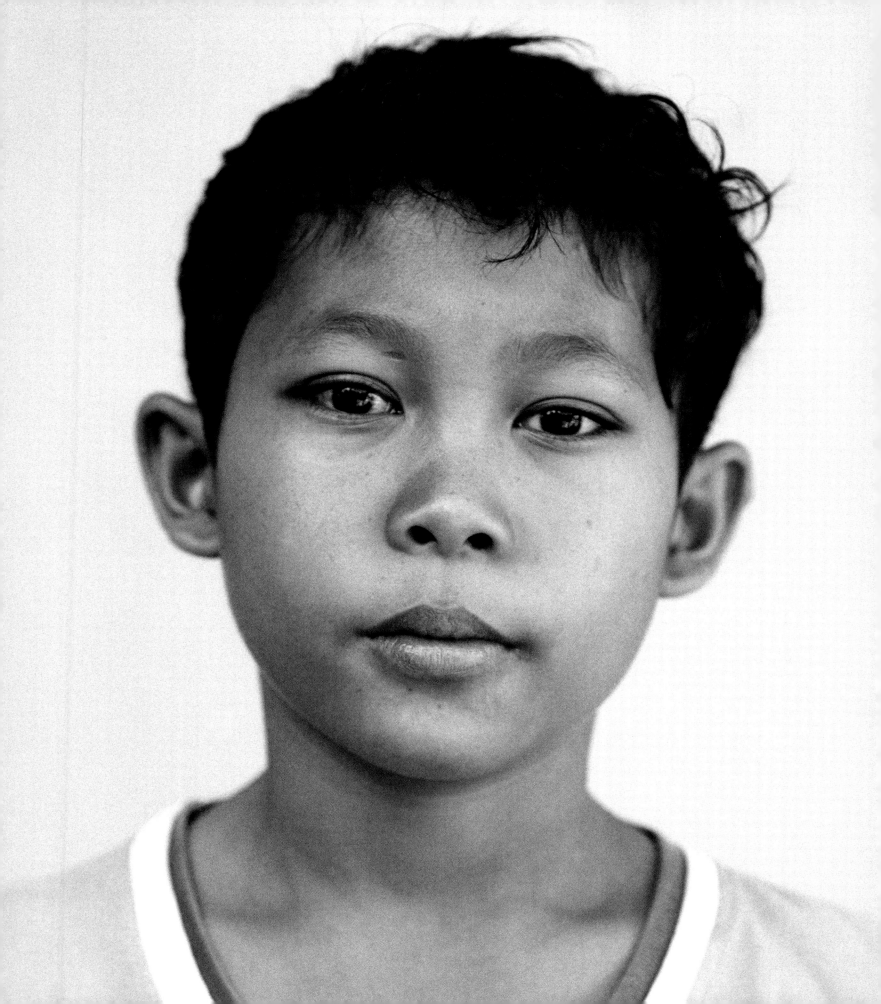

Jumna, 11 Germany

Robson, 12 Brazil

Rosa, 12 Germany

Asel, 12 Israel

Ni Wayan Lara, 11 Indonesia

Esraa, 12 Israel

Geraldine, 12 Brazil

Patricia, 12 Brazil

Moritz, 10 Germany

Zarah, 11 Germany

Seda, 11 Germany

Jasmin, 11 Germany

Nadar, 10 Sudan

Lisa, 12 Germany

Ruben, 10 Spain

I Komang Kari, 14 Indonesia

Gülistan, 11 Germany

Matti, 11 Germany

Jonas Roberto, 11 Brazil

Mats, 10 Germany

Amar, 11 Israel

Annika, 12 Germany

Dina, 11 Israel

Andrew, 13 England

Can, 11 Germany

Dilara, 11 Germany / **Alexia, 12** Spain

Anhang

Artist Statement

Die fotografische Arbeit für dieses Buch begann 2006. Der Schulwechsel meines ältesten Sohnes war der Auslöser. Neue Freunde, alle zwischen 10 und 11 Jahren, kamen in mein Blickfeld und regten mich mit ihrer Ausstrahlung und kribbeligen Weltsuche dazu an, sie zu portraitieren. Ich hatte das Gefühl bei etwas besonderem dabei zu sein und wollte diese Schwelle zwischen den Lebensphasen festhalten. Ich begann mich zu fragen, ob es dieses Moment zwischen den Welten, also zwischen Kindheit und Erwachsenheit, auch in anderen Ländern, Kulturen und Lebensbedingungen gäbe. So begann ich eine Art Fotoforschung in den Gesichtern von Kindern aus anderen Umgebungen und Zusammenhängen. Zwischen 2007 und 2014 nahm ich meine Hasselblad und viele Rollen Schwarz-Weißfilm auf jede Reise mit, um Situationen für Portraits zu suchen. Ich kreierte immer ähnliche Bedingungen beim fotografieren um einen seriellen Charakter und eine Vergleichbarkeit zu erreichen.

    Die meisten Jugendlichen begegneten mir unbefangen und ermöglichten mir, sie unverstellt und sehr offen im Ausdruck zu fotografieren. Ihre Medienprägung überlagerte zu diesem Zeitpunkt noch nicht ihre persönliche Ausstrahlung. Diese Ernsthaftigkeit und das Vertrauen, sich mir und der Welt ungeschminkt zu zeigen, erzeugten in mir Respekt für ihre Stärke und den Wunsch, diese Zauberkraft zu schützen und zu erhalten, zumindest im Bild.

    In diesem Buch versammeln sich 70 ausgewählte Portraits von Jugendlichen im Alter zwischen 10 und 14 Jahren. Die Aufnahmen entstanden auf vier verschiedenen Kontinenten und unter unterschiedlichsten Lebensbedingungen. Allen Portraitierten gemeinsam ist die Sehnsucht und Hoffnung auf gute Entwicklungsmöglichkeiten um ihr Potential zu entfalten und so in der Gesellschaft einen angemessenen Platz zu finden. Ich würde mich freuen mit meiner Arbeit die ein oder andere Tür aufzustoßen. Türen in Räume mit mehr Verständnis, Vertrauen und insbesondere Begeisterung für das Neue, was jede und jeder meiner fotografierten Jugendlichen in unsere Welt einbringt. Jeder auf seine Weise: Like all, but me.

Carolin Schüten

Carolin Schüten ist künstlerische Dokumentarfotografin. Sie studierte Sprachen und Fotografie in der Lausanne, London und Los Angeles. Sie lebt als freischaffende Künstlerin mit ihrer Familie in Köln. Der Mensch und seine Lebensumstände stehen im Mittelpunkt ihres Werkes. Sie arbeitete bei ihren anderen großen Themen: *Apartheid in Südafrika* und *Leben in der Trabantenstadt* mit öffentlichen, gewerkschaftlichen, sozialen Trägern und Institutionen und veröffentlichte Bücher (Schwarzer Alltag in Südafrika, Greno Verlag, Chorweiler Ansichten, Emons Verlag) zu diesen Themen. www.schueten.de

Vera King

Vera King ist Professorin für Sozialisationsforschung an der Universität Hamburg. Sie hat u.a. über Wandlungen der Lebensphasen Kindheit und Jugend sowie über psychische und soziale Entwicklungen von Heranwachsenden und über Wechselwirkungen von Kultur und Psyche geforscht. Sie gibt gemeinsam mit H.-Ch. Koller die Reihe *Adoleszenzforschung* bei Springer VS heraus, 2013 ist dort eine erweiterte Auflage ihres Buchs *Die Entstehung des Neuen in der Adoleszenz* erschienen. Weitere Publikationen und Forschungsschwerpunkte finden sich auf der Homepage von Vera King: www.ew.uni-hamburg.de/de/ueber-die-fakultaet/personen/king.html

Artist Statement

My work on the portraits collected in this volume began in 2006. It was that year that I began to notice certain visual changes in the 10 and 11 year old pupils at and around the school my own children attended in Cologne. Something about their charisma captivated me and I started making photographic portraits of adolescents in Cologne and its vicinity. It wasn't long, though, before I began to wonder if this moment I had been observing in the faces of these local youths, this moment of "inbetweenness"—between the two worlds of childhood and adulthood—could be found in other countries, cultures and life circumstances. So, in the years between 2007 and 2014, I took my Hasselblad and many rolls of black-and-white film on every trip, searching for opportunities to make more portraits. I always endeavored to create similar conditions for the photographs to give the images a serial character and maximize their comparability.

Most of the adolescents I photographed were unselfconscious and allowed me to capture them on film with a natural and very open expression. At this point in their lives, their individual aura had not yet been overshadowed by their awareness of medial impact on their developing selves. The earnestness and trust with which they revealed themselves —unmasked—to me and to the world earned my respect and cultivated my desire to protect and preserve this magic, if in no other form, at least as an image.

This volume encompasses 70 selected portraits of adolescents between the ages of 10 and 14. The photographs were taken on four different continents and their subjects come from a wide variety of life circumstances. All of the adolescents portraited here share the hope for opportunity, for the chance to develop their potential and find an appropriate place for themselves in society. It is my hope that this volume might open one or the other door—doors in spaces of greater understanding, trust and, especially, enthusiasm for the unique contributions each of these adolescents makes to our world. Each of them in his or her own way: Like all, but me.

Carolin Schüten

Carolin Schüten is an artistic documentary photographer. She studied languages and photography in Lausanne, London and Los Angeles. She lives with her family in Cologne, Germany, where she works as an independent artist. The focal point of her work centers on people and their life circumstances. She has been supported by public institutions, labor unions and social organizations for her previous work on apartheid in South Africa and life in the satellite city, which has been published as Schwarzer Alltag in Südafrika [Everyday Black Life in South Africa] (Greno Verlag) and Chorweiler Ansichten [Chorweiler Cityscapes] (Emons Verlag).
www.schueten.de

Vera King

Vera King is a professor at the University of Hamburg, specializing in socialization research. Her research focuses on the transformations associated with childhood and adolescence and on the psychological and social development of young adults, as well as on the interplay of culture and the psyche. She is co-editor with H.-Ch. Koller of the series Adoleszenzforschung [Research in Adolescence] published by Springer VS. An expanded edition of her book Die Entstehung des Neuen in der Adoleszenz [The Emergence of the New in Adolescence] appeared at Springer VS in 2013. Further publications and research activities are listed on Prof. King's homepage:
www.ew.uni-hamburg.de/de/ueber-die-fakultaet/personen/king.html

Max, 12
Venice Beach, USA 2008
Blanca, 12
Sollér, Spain 2008
Ariel, 10
Jerusalem, Israel 2009
Asram, 12
El Fasher, Sudan 2008
Carlos, 13
Sollér, Spain 2008
Romy, 12
Los Angeles, USA 2009
Michael, 11
Jerusalem, Israel 2009
Johan, 12
Sollér, Spain 2008

Paul, 11
Cologne, Germany 2007
Jona, 12
Cologne, Germany 2008
Hedda, 13
Cologne, Germany 2010
Lira, 10
Sao Paulo, Brazil 2009
Salim, 11
Cologne, Germany 2006
Charlotte, 10
Krefeld, Germany 2006
Ludwig, 11
Cologne, Germany 2007
Jina-Yi, 11
Los Angeles, USA 2008
Philippa, 11
Wissen, Germany 2007
Achmed, 12
El Fasher, Sudan 2009

Jordi, 11
Sollér, Spain 2008
Yossef, 11
Negev, Israel 2009
Cody, 12
Venice Beach, USA 2008
Luca, 11
Cologne, Germany 2006
Stefanie, 12
Sao Paulo, Brazil 2009
Abeer, 12
Negev, Israel 2009
Fabio, 12
Sao Paulo , Brazil 2009
Diani, 10
El Fasher, Sudan 2009

Shuk, 12
Negev, Israel 2009
Selma, 10
El Fasher, Sudan 2008
Ahed, 12
Negev, Israel 2009
Alham 12
Negev, Israel 2009
Mais, 12
Jerusalem, Israel 2007
Mohamed, 13
Negev, Israel 2009
Abdan,12
El Fasher, Sudan 2008
Oskar, 12
Sollér, Spain 2008
Halima, 12
El Fasher, Sudan, 2009
Jana, 10
Cologne, Germany 2006

Juman, 11
Jerusalem, Israel 2007
Alexa, 11
Los Angeles, USA 2008
Lara, 10
Cologne, Germany 2007
Ronnie, 12
Los Angeles, USA 2008
Melissah, 12
Cologne, Germany 2007
Clara, 12
Cologne, Germany 2008
I Kadek Rian, 12
Bali, Indonesia 2009

Jumna, 11
Cologne, Germany 2007
Robson, 12
Sao Paulo, Brazil 2009
Rosa, 12
Cologne, Germany 2010
Asel, 12
Negev, Israel 2009
Ni Wayan Lara, 11
Bali, Indonesia 2009
Esraa, 12
Negev, Israel 2009
Geraldine, 12
Sao Paulo, Brazil 2009
Patricia, 12
Ubatuba, Brasilien 2009
Moritz, 10
Cologne, Germany 2006
Zahra, 11
Cologne, Germany 2007

Seda, 11
Cologne, Germany 2007
Jasmin, 11
Cologne, Germany 2007
Nadar, 10
El Fasher, Sudan 2008
Lisa, 12
Cologne, Germany 2010
Ruben, 10
Morro, Spain 2010
I Komang Kari, 14
Bali, Indonesia 2009
Gülistan, 11
Cologne, Germany 2007
Matti, 11
Cologne, Germany 2007

Jonas Roberto, 11
Ubatuba, Brazil 2009
Mats, 10
Cologne, Germany 2007
Amar, 11
Negev, Israel 2009
Annika, 12
Cologne, Germany 2007
Dina, 11
Jerusalem, Israel 2007
Andrew, 13
London, England 2008
Can, 11
Cologne, Germany 2007
Dilara, 11
Cologne, Germany 2007
Alexia, 12
Sollér, Spain 2008

Impressum/Colophon

Copyright: Carolin Schüten, Cologne
Text: Vera King, Hamburg
Image Editing: Wolfgang Zurborn, Cologne
Book Design: Bastian Ruppik, Düsseldorf
Typeface: Maison Neue
Paper: Gardapat, 150 g/m²
Scans: Kontrast Lab, Cologne
Production: Druckerei Kettler, Bönen
Published by: Verlag Kettler, Dortmund, Germany 2015
www.verlag-kettler.de

ISBN 978-3-86206-514-1
© 2015, Photographer, Author and Publisher
Cover Illustration: Abdan, Lira, Paul

Special Thanks to: Rolf Schüten,
Stefanie Grebe, Vera King, Fifi Tong,
Petra Roith, Alicia Ching, Knut Detlefsen,
Rina Yitzhaki, Susanna Santos-Thomas,
I Nengah Sukaryasa, Kerstin Reich,
Luca und Moritz Schüten, Simone Schüten,
Thomas B. Hebler, Ly und Frédéric Dumas,
Richard Reisen, Bastian Ruppik, Kontrast Lab
and to all the adolescents pictured
in this book

VERLAG KETTLER